SEXUALITY AND SEDUCTION

Vladimir Zivkovic

Smashwords Edition

Copyright 2017

TABLE OF CONTENTS

INTRODUCTION

This text is written to disperse misconceptions about human sexuality. As always, I advise people to check the legitimacy of the creation. Nothing is accidental, and no action is without the consequences. This text should help the reader realize that there is no coincidental happiness, but only deserved one. That also means that happiness related to sexuality can't be arbitrary. It is the result of a pure, innocent and human sexuality. Who doesn't believe such claims, my advice is to check for validity of this reading at least. Still, it's always better to live properly and humanely, than to check for errors, faults, and sin. The results of errors are always: the waste of time and misery.

That's the truth that modern man has forgotten. Even worse thing is that there are a few of those a man can learn from the laws of Universe, which are happening every second faultlessly.

And why is that so?

It's because a man feels lonely and lost in Space. It's time to change this situation.

Chapter I – Sexuality – A short guide for dummies

PERFECT AND POSITIVE

God is perfect and everything He creates is perfect. Therefore all created has perfection within itself and has a perfect purpose.

What does this mean?

Souls are at different developmental stages. Thus they inhabit different bodies. Therefore each being has perfection within itself while only his thoughts and actions can vary from the worst possible to best possible ones.

Still, even the worst deeds entail perfection because the outcome of these deeds would cleanse and lead to the goal. In this way, you have right to free will, but you don't have right to randomly change the outcomes of the actions.

From the secular point of view, God is the only one who is perfect and everything else is imperfect.   Therefore, from the secular point of view, there are positive and negative actions. Positive actions results are mainly good while negative ones are insignificant.

It can be easily seen in the case of masturbation. If a person has no sex partner and wants to live its own sexuality, fairest solution is masturbation. While masturbating you may make two catastrophic mistakes which are not nearly bad as irresponsible sex relationships with other human beings. When it comes to masturbation, it is bad if you think about someone else's i.e. the person in the relationship. If you think about someone else's partner, then the consequences won't be good for you. Still, even in that state of desperation, if that other person that you are thinking about has clear mind and heart, it will be protected from your lecherous thoughts, so you will be the only one to suffer the consequences. Otherwise, the other person may be encouraged by your imagination, and he/she may have problems too. Still, I have to mention that events and problems that are the outcome of this case can't be desirable or positive, although many would like to think how can that be so, but not to happen in that manner. The other mistake is thinking about the single person. That is also wrong because that is an attack on another person's freedom and dignity.

So, when masturbating you have right to think about your partner or about an imaginary person if you need sexual gratification. Such doing, maybe isn't perfect, but it's very positive. That is because in such manner you achieve an extent of sexual gratification generally without doing much harm to anyone.

This could be explained by a straightforward example. The knife has a perfect purpose. One of them is to cut a slice of bread with it. If you cut yourself or others with a knife, then there is no slightest positivity in that let alone perfection.

A lesson is following:

Perfect acting brings happiness and true love. Positive acting brings self-satisfaction, the growth of love and joy.

Why do I say this?

In order not to be burdened by imaginary perfection; not to judge to self and others; not to commit sin by destructive sexuality as one thinks how fancy, able and modern he/she is.

AN IMAGINARY PERFECTION

One of the worst misconceptions of a man is to think as if sexuality is a sin.

What does that mean?

God created sexuality. He created the sexuality as an act of lovemaking and the way of continuation of the species. Sexuality as such has perfect nature. The other thing is that people use such wonderful gift in a negative way so that they correspondingly get miserable, sick and lonely.

If a man is disappointed by sexuality, he should think about its own behavior and dignity.

In the past, people suppressed the sexuality. That was due to the collective belief that it's bad. People have condemned themselves and the others so it has reflected very negatively to the human psyche and to their acts in the past. They were under pressure that they shouldn't live sexuality because it's bad and sinful, thus they condemned themselves to bad deeds and bad luck. Nowadays, it goes to the other extremes. Modern people think that they have right to have sex with whoever they like. As if the sex isn't a sin. They have forgotten about their and other people's dignity. They don't realize that disrespect for oneself and others are also disease, as well as suppression of sexuality. However, sex can be really sinful if you use it for sinful aims. It's very simple to come to such conclusion.

Having in mind that sex as everything else has its perfect purpose; this means that since the man can't achieve perfect sexuality instantly, he has to use sexuality in a positive manner. That means a man has right to live sexuality at a certain point of his life when it's got proper conditions to do so.

In order to acquire and meet such conditions, the effort is needed. It's all in vain, but everything has to be deserved and for all is required mental effort. You can't have regular sex if you don't know well or respect your partner. That takes effort and time. You can't have positive and satisfying sex if you haven't acquired responsibility when it comes to the happiness of your partner and responsibility for the possible children.

The positive purpose of the marriage is that you can have free and safe sex in a marriage and planning the family is your own will. Any other sexuality out of the marriage is more or less destructive for an individual. Also, children that grow in normal and sensible marriage without the unity of both parents greatly suffer, and the parents themselves suffer too.

Sexuality outside of the marriage results in very bad consequences. Sexuality is nowadays lived under the motive of a modern love relationships "boyfriend and girlfriend". And in the majority of cases that is not positive sexuality and many complain and are angry at such claims. In reality, people don't want to admit their irresponsibility and lack of dignity, and they don't admit that their 'modernity' is actually bigotry that they want so hard to hide not just from others, but also from oneself. For, the glorification of things bringing misfortune and pretending to be special by committing a sin can't bring you or assure you happiness or success.

The message is following:

Many say that sex is not sinful. I would add: a divine aspect of sex that's achieved by fidelity and love is a positive sex, and as such has a positive effect. Of course, some sex can be very sinful. Don't trust people that give such short and incomplete statements. It's not a coincidence that they are so stingy with words and that they say that the wise man is quiet. Because, if they had been smarter, they would know that a smart man says what should be said and how much it should be said.

THE NEGLECTION OF THE PARTNER

When a man is in search for happiness, it's completely logical that one day he will eventually reach spirituality. Spirituality is the path that man takes when a man needs God. Such man is disappointed in world and life, so he turns to God.

What does that mean?

There are many spiritual paths. God is only one.

That means that many are entrapped by Ego, so they think they are more spiritual that those living a secular life.

Since the sexuality is a topic here, we have to deal with it through this problem.

Many spiritualists opt for abstinence from sex. That is not so bad if you don't have a partner. If you are married, then you have obligation to take care of partner's wishes. If you don't live sexuality while someone lives it, that doesn't mean that you are better or more spiritual than that person. As we have already concluded, sexuality has positive application and as such it helps people on their spiritual way. That means that two coupled in their common and pure sexuality always make progress on their path to God. They never regress. Only those irresponsible and reckless in their sexuality regress. Those not consummating sex and thus thinking they are for it better than others also regress. That's a first class egoism. Neglecting partner for the imagined spirituality is egoism.

Just to make clear something that many spiritualists haven't explained until the present day.

Why do people want to repress sexuality?

The reasons are selfishness and will to power.

Sexuality is powerful, thus living sexuality takes so much life energy. If this energy is saved, it can be used to develop spiritual powers. However, you generally don't need spiritual powers. God protects you and takes care of you so that helplessness really doesn't exist, because who could feel helpless if has God beside oneself on one's side? In that case, a man can only look helpless or think that he/she 's helpless.

A man eager for spiritual progress and progress of spiritual powers actually gives up on love.

Even a sick man feels love. A man without strength also feels love. If you lose everything, the capacity to love is not lost. Likewise, a man that lives sexuality doesn't lose the feeling of love. It is only lost by the one who looks for an imagined more and better. Ha ha, do you leave a loved person, even your children, under the excuse that they drag you backward on your spiritual journey? How much egoism is blinding in this case?

The message is following:

Each person is on its spiritual path, even the worst ones. Denying and belittling of sexuality implies complexes and injuries that have to be cured. However, this doesn't mean that person who realized God wants to have sex. Avatar has no desire for sex and it's really foolish when people want to find the significant other for Christ. In the same manner, many people have mentioned Buddha's married life before He realized himself. That's very ignorant because if you don't eat bread anymore, you don't really need a knife to slice it. Degrading God and self-realization is also egoism and ignorance. Two people as a couple always reach the point when they consensually agree that they don't want anymore to have sex. That's perfectly natural process.

According to that, a person that openly and honestly lives its own sexuality is better than the person who saves sexuality by taking advantage of others and for its own spiritual powers.

CONTRACEPTION AND ABORTION

Contraception and abortion are integral problems related to sexuality.

What does that mean?

Every person that has sex comes into a situation that there is a chance to deal with this problem

Contraception is used for many reasons. It's used with the goal of decreasing a possibility of conception and to protect a man from sexually transmitted disease.

Certainly, the modern suppliers are dealing with statistics and possibility. So, in such cases, their statistics are insignificant, although they want to prove that it is.

If the thief is caught red-handed after the first robbery, and the second one is caught after the tenth robbery, then statistics that you get away from punishment for ten times has no significance. In both cases, you're 100% in trouble if the statisticians will say that the second one went well in 90% of cases. Specifically, it is worse if you get caught stealing for the tenth time, because it's very likely that your previous offenses will be exposed, so the punishment will be more rigorous.

What do I want to explain?

Ignorant people rely on contraceptives. Due to the consumption of contraception, they are easier to engage in sexual relations. In such situations, it is much more likely to get a sexually transmitted disease or become pregnant, because no contraceptive is 100% safe, which manufacturers hide. And if you have received a sexually transmitted disease or conception occurred, then it was likely to happen 100%, and not 5% or 3%.

Contraception is a wishful thinking of the modern man to live selfishly without knowing it and to destroy oneself and one's own life. People that use contraception out of the marital relationship want to avoid the consequences of their selfishness. Therefore such people take risk of developing severe illness or facing the "accidental" pregnancy. Thus people, who engage in irresponsible sexual relationships, also use contraception irresponsibly and use contraception for negative purposes. A person using contraception for negative purposes always has an excuse and always wants to present to the world how properly he conducts i.e. to show its valid reasons. Such people receive and suffer sexually transmitted diseases, sometimes terminal ones. They also face an unwanted pregnancy. Then, naturally, not did they used contraceptives wrong, but they also want to terminate, and great problems arise for participants in sex, as for an unborn child. At this point, severe traumas have been suffered by man's psyche.

Many people think that only women have been damaged by abortion. Nonetheless, even a cold and insensitive man is suffering severe consequences subconsciously, as well as by karma.

The message is following:

The contraceptives are a perfect invention for couples who have chosen one another, who married and decided to have sex, as to reduce the possibility of conception because in the given moment that isn't acceptable solution. In such cases even if conception and abortion happen, consequences can be timely neutralized and more or less acceptable.

Using contraception for the sake of living of egoism and as protection from disease, and abortion as the consequence of irresponsible sexuality, bring huge karmic problems and psycho-emotional issues. As it would be said in my country:

- A little music and lots of money.

In doing so, the music I have mentioned is shallow and heathen, i.e. destructive.

CONCLUSION

Practice positive, innocent sexuality, while improving love and fidelity, and don't worry. God rewards such people and never condemns them.

If you look at something and think that it is fine, and is done in sin, then you look bad. That is why you think that it's better for others than for you, and it's no wonder that you are always disappointed.

Believe in perfection of God and creation. Believe in purpose and benefits of God's gifts. Sexuality is one of those gifts. You have right to live it as it's appropriate for a human being. On the other side, you'll be in trouble. Believe me, with such laws – there is no favoritism, nor random luck.

Because, how many people you know that pray for mercy, but they don't get it? Because it's a lot, and they haven't given when they should give. Unfaithfulness, as irresponsible and sinful sexuality, is a denial of mercy and happiness to oneself and to others.

So far, that would be all about that.

The rest of the questions and stories related to spirituality and the life of the man you can find in my books coming out in sequels in Serbian and English as **''Return to God''(Men and Women, Love Relationships), "Modern Relationships"** and **''A Contemporary Spirituality''**.

Chapter II – Lectures/Discourse on seduction

SEDUCTION = SELF-DOUBT

The young are under great pressure nowadays, when it comes to sex.

What does that mean?

Many say that if you have been put under pressure, you would get stronger. However, many of those don't mention what is even more important: if you back down/give in under pressure, you will fall apart.

As you could see, if you are exposed to troubles and pressures, the end result could be manifold.

The same goes for temptation. The reflection about the committing the sin is already another kind of pressure. That kind of pressure is negative because if you give in to it, you will head to misfortune. If you don't succumb to it, you will be in the situation you should have been in without the stress (thus losing strength and time).

Your body and mind are not immortal. If you unnecessarily expose them to the pressures, you will lose their strength and durability/endurance/permanence. Everything that is put to excessive use, it lasts shorter. This means that the wisdom of a man is reflected in choosing those experiences, and therefore the pressures that will lead him to the meaning and purpose of life.

Why have I mentioned that the young are exposed to the pressures nowadays?

Because the pressure I'm talking about is not productive. It destroys them.

If a young man has found a 'girlfriend', many will wish to do likewise. This is because they think that this young man is not only happy, but also important. Young men nowadays are under great pressure because they are not burdened with respect and love towards women, but only with seduction and sexual intercourses. This kind of burden and pressure is the consequence of self-doubt. Young men are unhappy with themselves exactly because they have sexual intercourses and they don't respect themselves. However, because of the pride and such state of affairs in society, they pretend to be special and happy about these actions.

Since young people are essentially inexperienced, they gain experience in the wrong way, and accordingly, they are unhappy. At that point, they think that there is something wrong with them, or even worse, they think as if they are unfit because they don't achieve the happiness as others do. But, alas! They even don't know that the others are not really happy.

As we can see, here is also revealed the truth that I have been warning you about all the time. The truth is written within you. Faking and pride can't hide the truth and self-doubt that you could see in front of you. Thus, you better look for the truth that comes/surfacing out of you. Don't waste your time trying to comprehend the world and people. That is due to the people's capacity to pretend and lie. Jesus told that you will recognize such people by the works they do.

If you have done some wrongdoing that brought misery to you, then you should at least realize that the result is the same with other people. Never trust the illusion that it will happen differently for someone else for same doing or wrongdoing. God is fair-minded and objective in making his judgment. Everyone gets the same sentence for the same good deed or wrongdoing. Maybe karma or motives are different, thus it is difficult for a man to recognize that.

So, not that long ago, people were under sexual pressure because the modern conviction has been created that sex is the meaning of life, so they had to masturbate in " the worst'' case. However, they were even there under great pressure because it was put into their heads that the masturbation is a sin. Still, both masturbation and sex can be sinful, but not always, but only when they are used to violate dignity, integrity, and love of the man. This is how it came from suppressing sexuality to do abuse of sexuality, that is even worse. This already has been evident in the excessive increase in the number of divorces, changing partners, even in the one-night stands. There is the onset of collective misery and loneliness. Succumbing unfortunate flow of life and meaninglessness. Snatching material gains and living selfishness. That is what is left if you have given up on God and His love.

The message is following:

Self-doubt is the problem that you can hide from others, but not for yourself. If you think that you are miserable, try turning over a new leaf.

Many people believe that the success in the world and appraisal of others, fame, sex, power, and money will bring them luck. Don't be so naive. Start to believe that your misfortune is brought upon you by self-doubt because of which you have to do shameful deeds, be proud and prove yourself. Thus you better start praying and trust God. His concern and presence will diminish your self-doubt, so you will stop losing your esteem and dignity, trying to put up yourself and humiliate the others.

There is no worse self-doubt (and evil itself), from the wish to seduce. That sort of bigotry and pressure destroys self-respect and happiness of the young, and further on the old because the young become the old at some point.

EXPERIENCE IN SEX

Steer clear of the one who has lots of experience in sex, and it hasn't gained it with you.

To put it more precise:

– It's always better keeping your dignity.

Imagine someone who has experience in infidelity…

… and that is it.

SEDUCTION AND MANIPULATION

During my life (unfortunately) I often have the opportunity to see young girls ruined in a short time.

How does that happen?

The biggest problem is that no one warned these girls that seducing and manipulating are leading people to misfortune. It happens that a girl sees seduction by men as something normal and highly desirable. Then it happens that she answers in the same way to the male seduction and manipulation. By manipulating, the girl is actually ruthlessly used, without seeing that coming.

Under such circumstances, no relationship will survive. That is why is girl always trying again and again to make a new relationship.

This is the way how this girl gets ruined, in just couple of years.

Thus the woman has to keep her dignity and her faithfulness. She owns that to herself and her happiness.

THE ART OF SEDUCTION

Some men are nowadays considered to be great seducers. Many admire the skillful seducers, even women.

What does that mean?

That means that there are many women that don't recognize true values in men. For reason many admire egotistical seducers, there are many hearts broken nowadays.

However, in this presentation, I won't deal with the real seducers, except that I will say that they will get what they deserve. For those who don't know that, there are much more men that would like to be successful seducers. Their problem is just that they haven't mastered that skill.

What is this about?

At first, you want to be someone. Then you invest time and effort to be that someone. And you end up by paying off your wretchedness and sin, because what you have become stands for evil in the world and brings inevitable bad-luck. When I say inevitable, that means 100% will happen.

Therefore, learning to be a seducer, that is not only a complete waste of time, but it's also investing an enormous effort in your own and other people's misery.

It's a great sin to learn to seduce people.

Pray to God to protect you from such a way, and from this kind of people.

Chapter III – The examples of seduction (Note: this example can also be found in the other books)

HOW MUCH DO LOOKS MATTER?

We live in a time when the pleasure is highly valued. If one values pleasure too much, then much will be invested in things that bring pleasure. Thus they begin to value: looks, affluence, intelligence, science, and sex. Love and character, as well as God, is being neglected.

What does that mean?

Egotism and the human stupidities are one and the same thing. Stupidity destroys the character of the man, its dignity, and its capacity to love. That is generally reflected in the misery of a man that lives and acts in such manner.

Once there was a girl that had "something" that many men liked about her. She was really unattractive, but she always got to find "boyfriend". Because she was unattractive, she envied the girls that looked handsome. Because of her despise towards beautiful girls, she insisted on the conviction that the physical appearance is not important for the relationship between the man and the woman. That is why she convinced herself that the beautiful girls are not special and that they find the man thanks to their looks. She liked to think as if she was special, and has "something", because, although she is unattractive, she was always capable of finding a new "boyfriend".

One of her ex-boyfriends has found a new girlfriend that was really pretty. He said:

– No matter what kind of girl she is, I prefer beautiful one with flattering behind and boobs, just being without "something" that my unappealing ex-girlfriend has.

What is this about?

Many beautiful and attractive people have bad character and live promiscuously. However, many people with unappealing looks are the same. It is very negative if you are envious and hate good-looking people (also unattractive ones). The character of the man is the most important thing to look at. Envy and hatred are very negative personal traits, and they define how bad is some person. Thus pay attention to "something" that many are pointing out. What is it that is special according to their point of view? If someone is not admiring beauty, why is that so? Why would someone not appreciate something that someone else has?

The beauty is passing. However, that's the reason to appreciate and respect it more. Also, many other things are passing. Fame, power, money, etc. What matters about the false things is that they are transient. But if something is transient, that doesn't mean that you have to hate or despise it. If so, the ugliness is transient too. Certainly, the life will come in which you will have a beautiful body. It is not good to hate neither beauty nor ugliness. Any feelings related to that represent your karma for past actions. That means that your character determines both your physical appearance and your attitude towards it.

The message is following:

Many unattractive people are worse than the beautiful ones. That has to do with the character, not with the physical appearance. Thus the character of the person is not estimated according to its looks. A beautiful woman that had only one man is more faithful and dedicated than the one who had many. The same goes for a man (heh, it is strange everything that I have to write).

That's why the ex-boyfriend statement that I mentioned in the example is not strange at all. Manipulation of intelligence, money, convenience, looks, and genitals, can never be assumed as "something". Thus, take close look at positive dispositions that some person has and watch how he/she uses them. It is not bad to respect beauty and usefulness if the character is shaped like a diamond. However, those who don't have good dispositions badmouth the things that are not necessarily negative.

SUBURB

In the suburb of a city, a hunk of a guy moved in. The girls that were living there were much delighted when they saw him. He didn't pay attention to them. One of the girls from the neighborhood was very interested in him. She was not afraid to show him that. He, however, was not touched. She seemed funny to him. He had such attitude because he'd already had such experience.

What does that mean?

Some people grab the attention of the opposite sex just with their appearance. However, such people are faced with this from the earliest childhood. Nevertheless, these people realize that people who are impressed with the fake, i.e. with the thing that you're not, basically don't appreciate you and don't love you, and they don't have the slightest idea about who you are, or what kind of person you are.

Of course, from this point, I don't talk about narcissism. Narcissists hate others in a way that they adore their physical looks and consider it the most important. Here I talk about the realization of the man who has realized that the only important thing is that your potential partner takes interest in you, for what you really are, and not just for looks, material goods, abilities, and influence.

Many saints are teaching that praise doesn't enhance you, and that criticism doesn't break you. That's because the both of them deal with ego and complexes. Initially, you want to believe how special you are, so you're bothered with other people's opinion. Then you realize who you really are, and you know how much you're worth, so the shameful seduction of others makes you laugh. It exactly makes you laugh, and not angry, or enlightening you. Because, the one who knows Self, knows that potential partner must see real him/her if he is really interested in it and its personality.

Here we can realize why sex addicts are bad with the opposite sex. That's because they are interested in fake. That's because they present themselves falsely, so exactly these people are astounded how "fool" or "sissy" gets the girl.

Here I want to note that this tendency of man has its roots in parents. Children subconsciously acquire lots of things from their parents, and often the worst things. Finally, many people hate traits of a parent which are actually the traits of the child from the previous lives.

The message is following:

Find your value so you don't yield to seducers and those who don't know who you really are, and what kind of person you are. Because, it's a great delusion when people treat you like undivine being, and you think how special you are because the fanatics are cheering to you. Therefore, don't yield to seduction. Love yourself and your heart.

DESPERATION IN LOVE

Nowadays, women and men, instead of learning from each other, they fight among themselves.

What does that mean?

Many women don't realize that men are principled. They don't like if a woman acts badly. Women are emotional. They don't like when a man's brutal.

In this story, certain women are the topic, thus we will commit to that. The story goes on:

A woman has fallen in love with a man. The woman acted lasciviously. The man didn't like that and he was withdrawn. When she noticed that he is withdrawing, she used the art of seduction. That has made the man withdraw even more. The desperate woman had found another man and hoped that the one she liked was going to be jealous.

One day, these two have met. He was still alone. She told him that he deserves a good wife. She was thinking that about herself. He knew that, but he was playing stupid. He thought to himself:

– God, is it possible that such women exist- women that do evil every second? Is it possible that she has an affair with another man and still, thinks about me? Does she still think how she loves me, and how good is she?

The message is following:

Don't trust people who think that they have right to love one person and to sleep with another one. Don't trust those who commit sin from ''love''.

DRAMA

A girl fell in love with a man at her work. She entrusted both her male and female friend with her secret. They laughed at her. They told her that the man is worthless. She was ashamed. She also overlooked the truth that no man is worthless, especially if he inspires noble feelings in someone. She also didn't realize that her friends laughed at her because they didn't take her feelings seriously.

A man whom she liked was not at all being aware what was going on.

Soon afterward, the rest of the colleagues at work observed that she liked him. Since she was beautiful, they were very envious and jealous. Joined together, they used every chance to keep her away from him, while she was trying to get closer to him. The man turned out funny in their presence. How not to be funny, if everyone has humiliated him at the workplace?

However, this girl didn't notice that her colleagues are traitors, but she thought how extraordinary they are because they're so smart and capable. This situation was very painful for her because she thought how stupid she is because she liked such a clumsy man. She was crying.

The man that she had liked still had no idea about that.

Everyone knew about her feelings for him.

He still didn't know anything.

Then, the disappointed girl started drinking and loafing around, and she ended in bed with another man, whom she didn't love. She was broken. She felt unloved.

The man whom she was in love with still didn't know anything.

And how could he know if she hadn't entrusted that to him? She disclosed her innermost feelings to fools, and not to whom she should. Why and how could he know, if she was hanging around with those who belittled him and even if she had confessed to him he wouldn't trust her?

The message is following:

Many women are known for gossip. However, to reveal one's feelings to someone who shouldn't know about it, and hiding one's feelings from someone you mustn't, equals to suicide.

Many men are fooling around and pretending as if they knew everything. Thus, many aren't sure about anything until you say them so. Even then they suspect, although they fake confidence. That's because the man is thinking much more than the woman. That's the reason he has doubts. Women think that they're the only fragile.

For that reason, a woman should disclose intimacy only to a man she truly loves. She also has to be sincere. Female sincerity is the greatest gift to the man. There are no charms that can impress him as devoted feelings. Many women know that.

In this instance, it's not only important woman's sincerity to the man she loves. This example implies that when the woman's in bad company, not that she can't get the man whom she loves, but she also goes astray with time, so she becomes unfaithful and evil, and she imagines how unfortunate in love she is. More precisely, as weird as it sounds, love of the women described here – was not sincere (that is not love because love isn't like that).

THIS IS MY GIRLFRIEND (Aka, a cautionary tale to reflect on)

Once, a man went to the bank of Danube to sunbathe. He was sitting near the water and enjoying. Not far from him, he saw a girl with a man. They were holding and kissing each other. The man said to her:

– You're my girl.

After a while, the man has left. Not long after that, another man came. He was also holding and kissing her. He told her:

– You're all mine.

Then he also left.

The girl approached the man that was sunbathing. She told him:

– Everyone says that I'm their girl.

The man has answered:

– That's because your answer is always "yes". That's the same as your answer's always "no".

Then the girl asked him:

–What are we going to do? Are we going to take a bath?

He answered:

– I'm sorry. It's too late to bathe and look at my pants how clean and shiny they are.

Then the young man saw God bent over the surface of Danube, pouring water from one hand into other.

Chapter IV – Delusions on Sexuality

SEX WITH NO STRINGS ATTACHED

Many things in the world and life very often happen just in someone's mind. When one looks the same thing from the side, it will come to the conclusion that many people live in illusions.

What does that mean?

That mainly means that people are twisting a lot, so they distort both reality and truth. Exactly these people consider themselves realistic (especially men).

A person makes a conclusion in various ways. The worst is if you live on assumptions. The one thing is if you have to do something so you have to figure out everything that could happen. In that case, the assumption can be helpful. The other thing is if you deny everything around you and interpret it as matching to egoism. Because of the selfishness of the modern ego and its constant desire to be smart and special, there are lots of misconceptions nowadays based primarily on assumption, and further on denying the world and its laws. Those who often deny reality are the people who are only looking for material things and facts. Such people deny spirit, energy, inner vision and God itself. If they just stand off for a bit, it's because they got some impression that energy, thoughts, and emotion exist, so they must acknowledge it.

That's how emerged concepts such as "friends with benefits", and "sex with no strings attached". It even goes so far in the disregard of existing concepts, it is believed that you can have friendly sex with someone, with no strings attached, and then when you have found a partner, you will end an agreement, and make-believe, nothing happened!

Of course, this is a serious misconception of the mind. Every normal person knows that every action has its reaction. The very idea about the sex with no strings attached being favorable situation for someone, implies selfishness, irresponsibility, debris, and desire to do evil things without a repayment, what is, honest to say– severe ignorance, because, that is as equal as when you have eaten an apple and you believe you would not have to digest it, and that you are so special so you would not have to pass it by defecating.

Today, I simply want to explain that sex with no strings attached is a fabricated idea that doesn't really exist. It exists only in disillusions of the mind. If you are having sex with someone, you are obliged by karmic laws. You are forcing it upon yourself. There is no running and avoiding the law. Also, if you think that you are having sex with someone as a friend, in that way you just show that you are not his/her friend at all. True friends help and respect each other. Sex with no strings attached is irresponsible and implies disrespect for oneself and the person you have sex with. There can't be mention of friendship, without it being a lie.

The message is following:

The friends with benefits is a concept that doesn't exist. There is no such thing as sex with no strings attached. The sex itself is already obliging. Thus, one should not confuse this terms, because it brings lies and confusion. There is a sex when one wishes that it is not obliging. However, such wish can't is ever fulfilled.

Many spiritualists say that it is all possible for God and that He could make any wish come true. From the example, we see that is not always realistic to believe in such thing. God can fulfill any wish. Still, He will not pass by the laws of Cosmos He himself has established. Therefore, the wish is in vain, i.e. it is not possible to fulfill it in the way you would like if it goes against the laws of creation. God does not fulfill every desire precisely because He is perfect and omnipotent. If He use his own omnipotence to satisfy human stupidity and egoism, the world would not be ideal for the development of the soul.

Therefore, trust that God can fulfill every your wish which is in accordance with your development and the development of others. Otherwise, you will believe in blunderings and illusions. The life of blundering and illusions is a life of disappointment and loneliness.

Thus, if you often get disappointed in the others or in life, think about that: isn't the problem with you?

Because I have just explained that non-existing concepts such as "friends with benefits" and "sex with no strings attached" are a reality for some people and they often use them in their mind and in their speech. They even try to live them, as if it is possible!

Hehe, it is possible, but without the benefits (with uncomfortable consequences) and with responsibilities. Why they then express themselves differently, and thus confuse many other people?

TANTRA

From the East, and especially from India, many different teachings came to us.

What does that mean?

India is a country where the people are raised in such way that most of them have a place for God. That means that India is modern Mecca of spirituality. From there came many useful and positive spiritual disciplines. Also, there are many good and true spiritual teachers in India. In the other countries, they are rare (at least not of that capacity).

Still, many times I have pointed out, and I will keep warning you about that. There is a black sheep in every flock. Thus it's not bad to mention that there are many false spiritual teachers in the East. That means that there is the greatest number of wrongly directed spiritual techniques.

One of them that I will mention here is "tantra". By its origin, that is the discipline that entails the sex and the partner with the aim of being united with God. Certainly, the idea itself is a failure. However, due to the new wave of sexual so-called freedom, people all over the world were greatly interested in this technique. That is because tantric teaching went so far in a negative direction that the rule was established that all must have sex with each other in such institutions because a woman is "joni" that must be respected. Therefore, No one has to be offended or to refuse the person of the opposite sex (hehe). And this reminds me of Hue Heffner's philosophy that has a lot of similarities (once again, hehe). You humiliate and destroy yourself and women on all possible levels and you are saying that woman should be respected?

Also, lately I notice that wherever there are trials in the courthouse too much attention is given to the facts and evidence while the injuries of the soul are overlooked. So it happens that woman gets divorced and goes away with another man while the abandoned man is treated as aggressive and jealous. I am the most surprised by the fact that if the woman is already with another man, isn't that good enough proof that man had reason to be jealous and mistrusting and that he suffers from typical injury of his heart and soul?

On the other side, if a man acts in that manner, women ignore that, which is even more strange.

So, here I am again explaining the importance of loyalty and dignity. All my teaching consists of continual repetition and pointing to these values and necessity of the same.

Very few people know that there are two directions in Tantra. This other direction has exceeded sexuality as a possible way to be united with God.

How did that happen?

Simple . There are always people who are honest in their search and what prevents them from progress on their way to God awakes them and puts off of that. Thus one shouldn't judge quickly when someone says he/she is tantric, because that doesn't mean that sex is necessarily used, but it can easily be the other way round, that such person has opted for celibacy, yoga, mantra, and meditation.

As we can see, tantra (although I would rather say and advise, common, simple sex) can be useful for some time in marriage, if you practice it only with your partner. Still, even such sexuality at the threshold of the old age must go away, because that's the natural process.

Therefore, if you have sex with more people, you will lose your dignity. Many tantra practitioners lie themselves and others that there is no sign of jealousy in their practices of tantric sex. That's the lie. The man is not an animal so that he can be trained to such unfaithful and insensitive way, but the other way round, he should turn more sensitive. Sexuality is powerful and divine energy that has a positive effect only in loyalty and dignity. Changing partners or using a partner through sex for the purpose of fictitious union with God is the misconception. It's a simple desire for pleasure and powers which is not an integral part of the spiritual path. An unfaithful man betrays, and inevitably creates injuries and jealousy. God and love are automatically pushed into the other plan, i.e. there is no chance for them to come into focus.

The message is following:

As we could see, an attractive way turns out to be the worst possible one. Respect the perfect teacher, but at the same time be alert to the buffoons who are more numerous in their ignorance and deception. So, never trust those who have more than one sex partners. Neither in their happiness nor in their love. Let alone believing in such spirituality. It is all lies and misconceptions of the mind.

OEDIPAL COMPLEX

Many things are focused on sexuality in the modern world. Because of the excessive, and I must say unnecessary forcing of sexuality, much of things is misinterpreted and evaluated wrongly.

What does that mean?

Because science and intelligence are very admired, many like to apply psychology and to interpret characters and behaviors. Of course, I must point out that this is done completely wrong.

Therefore the Edip's complex is considered to be an exclusively sexual problem.

Freud was a great psychotherapist. However, we shouldn't forget that he was the contemporary in the society where the sexual revolution was very cherished. That means that he was obsessed with sex like many of his contemporaries so that he associated many things with sex, although it didn't have to do anything with it.

Likewise, the Oedipal complex is having very wrong interpretation nowadays. Still, I must state that Oedipus complex is very much present nowadays. That means that it exists in excess, but it is badly treated and cured.

Oedipus complex has much to do with mother, i.e. with the connectedness of son and mother and not with sexuality as it is thought. When Oedipus has discovered that he was married to his mother and that he had sex with his mother, he blinded himself. Thus many people associate Oedipus complex with sex. However, the truth is completely different.

If the man hasn't grown up, he is always mama's boy. Such man is very often incapable of success in the world and his relationships with women are not relationships, but connectedness similar to a mother-son relationship. That's why immature man tied to the mother is never going to have a healthy and normal love relationship. He links connectedness to mother and lack of closeness to a mother with a woman he is in a relationship with thus he has to bear with such relations. If such man has no wife or girlfriend, he always ends up with his mother. That is because the mother doesn't allow her son to be independent, she is not raising him well and she makes the catastrophic mistake that many modern women don't see as a mistake, and that is that they criticize father and represent him in a negative way. Mothers that support Oedipus complex in men- their sons, and in that way bring misery to their sons, teach sons that their father is bad and they shouldn't look upon him when it comes to character.

That is very harmful because in that way son loses the male principle and the support in life thus he becomes incapable of career and love with the opposite sex.

Therefore, the Oedipal complex is closely connected with the spirituality of the man. If a man doesn't direct his look towards God or to his inner self, it is almost sure that he will become mama's boy in this modern time. Because, the negative battle between sexes was never so strong, present and devastating as today.

Many women started to recognize this negative disposition of the men, so mama's boys became despised in female company. However, it is very strange that women are driving forces and creators of mama's boy. They subconsciously, but on purpose create mama's boy that later on destroys them in love relationships.

The message is following:

Oedipus syndrome has lots to do with the bad connection between son and mother with lack of closeness between son and mother and then son and father, that has to be born because the mother is not playing the true and decisive role in the life of her son. Therefore, the Oedipal complex has very little to do with sexuality between son and mother because the love and closeness are not determined by sex and lust.

THE ABUSE OF HUMAN BEING

If a man wants prostitution services, he will have to pay with money. The money that the person sets aside to pay sex services supports the survival of the prostitution chain.

What does that mean?

Those who organize a chain of prostitution gain bad karma. Still, those who also support the survival of that chain with money or in some other way, also gain bad karma.

The same situation is with modern television shows, especially with the reality show. Those who organize the reality show gain a very bad karma. Nevertheless, those who watch, and especially those who vote, support with their money not only the public broadcast of the fornicators' actions, but also justifying the situation of people being treated as cattle and for putting money and salaries into the reserve houses and yards, wherein this way they destroy: their dignity, integrity and the possibility of a sublime life.

As I have put it here, if a man uses his mind, he will understand. However, there are many other relations where people don't understand, nor they can understand that something is simply bad. On the contrary, they have lots of suffering to survive, stumble and think. I will try to explain this with an example.

A young girl had left many relationships behind her. She has never been 'alone'. After she has broken up with a man, she will straightaway begin another relationship.

It happened that she was alone, a and she immediately fall in love with another guy. She used her friends to get to know what he thinks about her. The surprise was great, he said that he wouldn't even dream of being in a relationship with her because she is not a reliable woman when it comes to a relationship. He used her promiscuity and constant change of partners as the explanation.

She was very angry when she found that out from her friends. When she had found out that from her friends, she has been very angry. Secretly she blamed him as if he lacks respect for her and how he talks bad about her. She immediately has found a new man, although she was still in love with the first one besides being offended. She was telling to the second man as if the other man lacked respect for her and considered her an easy woman. This new man who dated you started to hate the first one. Secretly, he was also mad at him.

One day, this girl's friend was talking to a guy she was previously in love with. She told him that she is a decent girl and criticized him for considering her friend easy.

Then the man said:

– It is not about what I think and feel about her. Her actions are such that there is no man that could rely on her. If my opinion was so bad, I would have slept with her. It is more obvious that man having sex with her is the one who doesn't respect her and considers her easy.

Indeed, the man who dated her failed her in the end.

The message is following:

One of the most frequent reasons for divorce today that people almost don't notice is taking something that firstly shouldn't be taken away from the person you "truly love". That is sex (and often the marriage, too) with someone you shouldn't have anything common. That is also the reason why many people in the old age stay alone and lonely inside, without the emotional support of the partner and without the feeling of God as Self within oneself.

Here we can make a parable as compared to prostitution example. If a potential partner doesn't respect oneself, that doesn't mean that you have right not to respect him-her. That means that woman is not made easy by men's judgment, but with her actions. So it is that woman is more often considered easy by the man who is having sex with her and takes away her dignity, and not by the one who talks straightforwardly what he thinks and feels.

The indifference is huge when someone thinks to have rights to buy love and sexuality with money.

That means that hard fate affects the men who under the disguise of "love", power and money take advantage of women. The same is for those who support prostitution with their money or mess with people in reality shows.

ONE NIGHT STANDS (aka, mutual raping/abuse)

One of the most common misconceptions nowadays is a belief that the one who reached the greatest pleasure, has accomplished the goal of life.

What does that mean?

If the man turns his back both to love and God, then he is left only with transient things. The most tempting of all transient things is a pleasure.

Weak people who are afraid of love admire mostly the pleasure. Enjoying sex is very tempting to such people and that is the main reason why many chose seduction. When it comes to seduction, it is respected how short it took you get him-her into bed and how much pleasure you take by having sex with her-him.

Thus nowadays there is the bigoted conviction that one night stands are very desirable in the life of each person.

Mind thinks:

-I can have tots of partners if I have one night stands and there is no need explaining that to anyone, in addition to that, I can brag and appraise my achievements.

However, the pleasure you have achieved is gone. So what's the goal you have reached if it lies in past? And that's not the all. Who thinks ever that he can save love, happiness, dignity, and self-respect with one night stands?

The answer is:

– The man who is alien and disgusting to oneself.

The person who sleeps with the stranger is the stranger to oneself. If you are having sex with the person you don't love, you are closing your heart completely.

What kind of person is capable of having one night stands?

The answer is:

An unhappy seducer.

So how it's then possible for the seducers to be so much admired in the modern society if it is obvious from the start of this presentation how dangerous people they are, and very miserable indeed?

How is possible that people give up on themselves and their happiness so much so they strive to seduce others?

The next thing.

Seduction of the man is never that devastating as for a woman. Girls are taught seduction from the young age. They experiment with their attractiveness and charms, so when the attack happens or even abuse or rape, no one realizes how that happened. Nowadays rape is taken for granted. The act of raping is very ignorant and so bad that the one who is raping has to become a victim at some point. I have personally watched in the working place how many women working in various institutions were being psychologically abused easily. Because the line between sex and raping is thin, then the line between communication and psychological abuse barely exists. It is publicly accepted (and lame) conviction that every man has a right to psychologically abuse any woman. It's a terrible fact that modern women are involved in the seduction game with men so mutual abuse is no longer imagination, but the reality.

Men and women have dates and one-night-stands, and this is nothing than the consensual rape. Sleeping with the stranger is neither good nor useful, although in the mind and the thinking this idea seems remarkable.

Even if the powerful pleasure happens in the one-night stands, this event burdens people in the future and all their future relationships, so such person not only do lives in past, but even his dignity is undermined and destroyed. Such person does it deserve that because he/she doesn't value oneself, one's own body, neither own heart, nor happiness.

The message is following:

One night stand destroys your heart and your happiness, undermine your dignity so that you will never again appreciate yourself. Chasing for pleasures is not the purpose of life. Enjoying the power of pleasure and always striving for new and stronger pleasure is the first line egotism that leads a man to loneliness, sadness, and misery. Those who insist on seduction and pleasure don't know themselves, they are strangers to themselves, therefore they believe that sex with a stranger could be useful and good.

However, any action has a reaction, so if the action is selfish and inhumane, such reaction will come back upon someone someday as a boomerang. Many people are forgetting that God is omniscient and omnipotent. That means that what you secretly do maybe couldn't be seen by anyone, but God certainly sees that (and karma itself). Thus, no wrongdoing could ever pass without the punishment.

A piece of advice:

Beware of temptation when you think that nobody knows what you are doing when you think that no one sees you, and when you think that nobody can find out what you have done. That certainly is not the truth.

INDECISION

A man went into a shop. A beautiful girl was working there. When he saw her, he thought that he had never before seen such beauty. Still, he was not distressed. He had so many times seen before a beautiful girl, and none of them have noticed him. That man was intelligent and interesting, but he didn't have a good opinion about himself. Thus he couldn't have noticed that she liked him.

The girl was in love with him. Because of his insecurity, he kept her subconsciously at the distance. Much time passed by. That girl had survived lots of things inside her. He didn't know that. Very often she was quarrelsome with him because she was angry about his not paying attention to her. Due to that, he became even more reserved, even if he adored her.

The girl had many suitors. Nevertheless, she was experienced enough, so she realized that men were mainly interested in her beauty and curves. Thus she also didn't have a good opinion about herself, what the man whom she liked made even worse with his passivity.

She thought how intelligent and beautiful this man was. Why should he take interest in her, when she's not interesting, besides attracting playboys?

Thus she didn't assume that he liked her. The single thing two of them did – created an irresolvable condition in terms of clarification and relationship.

She already had a broken heart.

One day, the young man looked at her and it seemed to him that he saw love in her eyes. Then he thought to himself – Maybe she likes me? How's that possible? – However, she looked at him in that way because she had decided to give up on him and continue with her life.

She started avoiding him. Because of pain, she even had changed her job. They stopped seeing each other. She found someone, while he was suffering for a long period.

What's the point of this story?

Every person is exceptional at something. You are, too. There's no doubt. When someone is better at something from you, then accept the reality. Still, every person has equal value as a human being in God's eyes. No one has right to diminish or humiliate oneself. This two people from the example did that all the time, and they failed and were miserable all the time, although they were exceptional individuals.

The story I've told happens every day in the world, and for some people, it happens all the time.

Many women think that men are the one to make the first step. Still, exact the same women tease and seduce men in the incorrect way so that they would notice and make the first step. The one who wants something is to ask for it. It's certainly nice when you like someone and he/she recognizes it and makes the first step. Still, not all people have good observation and good intuition. You have to be straightforward with some people.

Therefore, if the people appreciated themselves, they wouldn't come into such situation. The question is: why happened that these two from the story had such destiny?

Because they are not persistent they have respect neither for themselves nor for others, and they don't have faith in God and true love. They're similar to those who: sting and run.

Many think that this is the man's trait. That's not the truth. Women are actually those that act in such manner. They sting the heart and run away.

And why they run?

Because they've forgotten that their place is next to the man they love. They think that it's good for the man to run after them. Afterward, they wonder, how come that they are used?

Well, they're used because they haven't chosen their man, and because they're neither honest nor faithful to them, and because they think that man should assume their wishes and wants, and yet make the first step. As if the first step of a man will recover their dignity?

LUST

If love had to do with personal appearance and beauty, then mothers with ugly children wouldn't love their offspring.

What does that mean?

If someone doesn't know love, it can learn it from mothers.

Parents and children are linked by karma and they hurt each other very often. Though a child can be ugly, evil and sick, and mother will still love him/her. That means that present relationships between men and women are mainly based on lust and interest, not on love. Here I just want to point out that love between partners should exist and has nothing to do with looks or material state.

The man usually gets excited visually, and woman tactile. Therefore women that dress provocatively are evil and unfaithful. The man who take advantage of every chance to touch women, and meaning several different women, are unfaithful and irresponsible men.

What this men and women have in common?

It's common that they don't have respect for themselves, so for that reason, they don't respect the opposite sex, so they take advantage of their position.

Which position?

They take advantage of the same position that allows them to dress provocatively, to touch and seduce someone. Therefore, I always repeat that seducing is trait related to people with complexes that don't know love. Their success in seducing is very important to them because they have low self-esteem.

Therefore, Don Juans are never satisfied, nor happy. They exactly have evidence of being unfaithful. They know how much their victims are unfaithful. Why do I say, victims? There is no love relationship in seducing. There's only seducer and the one that's been misled. They are constantly taking turns in changing their roles. The victim becomes a despot and vice versa. Thus seducer never respects neither himself nor his victims. It's because he cheats, he doesn't love those who cheats on, because what kind of person is the one that is tricked and led into bed by seducer?

What am I explaining here?

Today, when a girl looks good, she's noticed by the most of the men for her looks. And if such girl succumbs to temptation and has so-called "boyfriends", there's growing contempt inside over the time, and results in her inability to surrender to love.

There's no wonder that modern girls dress up so scarcely and seductive. Such attire is the consequence of girls' unconscious revenge. Most girls deliberately provoke lust in men, unconsciously, or out of revenge, because they're not respected as human beings, but as hunks of good meat. A naive modern man thinks that they're doing their best for him. Such man is not realizing that provocative dressing is often the outcome of subconscious contempt that woman carries inside in the same manner as lack of self-worth and self-respect.

A woman in love hides her charms only for her man i.e. spouse, because she knows intimacy, loyalty, and trust, and knows its values.

I'm not accusing women in this presentation. It might be even said that I defend them. Nowadays hardly any man could understand the misfortune of the woman that wants to love and be loved, but she only comes across the men who want to sexually abuse her, while they shamelessly lie how much they love and respect her. However, the real truth is usually that even if she was ugly, that man wouldn't just dislike her, but he would also be disgusted by her.

Thus happens that contemporary women have to make effort to seduce men. They hadn't been left any other choice.

Poor men are in the similar position, which, if they are noticed for their physical appearance when women see that they are poor, they turn bad. What a pity!

The message is following:

If someone doesn't respect you, don't mess with him. If someone tries to seduce you, run as far as you can. If you are seducing, think twice about yourself.

This should help you learn that it's wrong for a woman to be provocative in public and that only unfaithful woman thinks that it's good for man to take initiative when it comes to physical contact. There's no wonder that many have eventually made the conclusion that they have contempt for the opposite sex, and they've never felt love.

Unfortunately, those who still haven't recognized the truth will be unfortunate in love relationships.

IMPORTANCE OF FEELINGS

Many people nowadays live as if the sex and money are the most important things in life. Materialism is rapidly increasing nowadays. Though, there are people that think that only feelings matter.

What does that mean?

The feelings are important. Although, it is not reasonable that everything in your life depends on feelings. That means that if everything depends on them, then there is no wonder that you feel unhappy. And if you are unhappy, what kind of feelings you could have?

This means that the people that think that feelings are important also live with the illusion that everything has to be good and perfect in their lives. That is how attachment and egoism are developed. This is how developed attachment to family, sex, money, children, pets, comfort and more...

Here is raised the question: how and why is that so?

That is because if your feelings matter so much to you, then you are not interested in the deeper meaning of something. Something happens to you, and you don't think about the significance of events, and why something happens to you, about the way to spiritually grow and become happy, but you think to yourself: – Poor me, I am so unhappy! – That is egoism itself that results in misery and misfortune.

When someone dies, people don't consider why that is beneficial, they think about how to end their attachment and how ruined, tricked and injured they are. And why is that so?

The reason is that people consider themselves pathetic, and depending too much on feelings and pleasure. Love is an integral part of life, and love is free, unattached, and everyone can live it. The main problem is that many don't live it, so they think it should be a gift from heaven.

What do I really point out here?

Men related to pleasure and easiness fosters selfishness, abandons love, while he believes that love is really important to him.

Also, the love feeling is not the only feeling.

The real trouble is that people find attachment more important, not the love. In that way a man thinks that God is cruel because he created suffering and death, not realizing that suffering and death are inevitable in creation. That is self-pity. Thus people that care about feelings, don't actually live love, but the worst selfishness. They don't live for love (although many won't trust this), and, of course, they can't perceive underlying reasons of incidents, suffering, and pain, they don't understand the world around them, they can't accept the world and people as they really are, and they believe as if they live for love and that they know love.

Thus, they live for selfishness, attachment, pleasure and belittled feelings, while they believe that they know love and live for it. Specifically, they live for love, but neither they have ever found it, nor lived it.

Some people really don't understand opposite sex at all, not their partner, and they think as if they know something about love.

It is hard to explain the things I present here.

Nowadays, women mainly glorify their feelings. Yet, exactly these women are lazy to deserve and get real and true love and positive feelings. They live insensitivity, infidelity, and self-destruction, while they are not interested in real reasons of creation and search for God. The question is if something brings misfortune, and you imagine that it brings happiness, does that mean that your happiness is going to be lasting? And is possible for fabricated truth to become reality, i.e. real truth?

The message is following:

Love feeling is important feeling. Though, besides love, there are many other binding and destructive feelings. Many modern men and women confuse these destructive feelings for love. They are so overwhelmed with the importance of their feelings that they are overlooking living egoism and selfishness in reality, and not love. That is manifested through bad luck in love relationships and through sufferings reflecting the lack of understanding of life, creation, and God.

In simple words, no one has right to be evil and unfaithful and make excuses with "love feelings". Because, this is, of course, hypocrisy and lie. You can deceive yourself and people on the secular, but you can't deceive God and karma.

www.ingramcontent.com/pod-product-compliance
Lightning Source LLC
Chambersburg PA
CBHW050525290526
45786CB00007B/2696